From the Flyers Novice AE Team

I Love My Hockey Mom

To All Hockey Moms with Love and Thanks

KPk
Key Porter Kids

Toronto, Ontario, Canada

THE CANADA COUNCIL | LE CONSEIL DES ARTS
FOR THE ARTS | DU CANADA
SINCE 1957 | DEPUIS 1957

ONTARIO ARTS COUNCIL
CONSEIL DES ARTS DE L'ONTARIO

The publisher gratefully acknowledges the support of the Canada Council for the Arts and the Ontario Arts Council for its publishing program. We acknowledge the support of the Government of Ontario through the Ontario Media Development Corporation's Ontario Book Initiative.

We acknowledge the financial support of the Government of Canada through the Book Publishing Industry Development Program (BPIDP) for our publishing activities.

KPk is an imprint of
Key Porter Books Limited
Six Adelaide Street East, Tenth Floor
Toronto, Ontario, Canada M5C 1H6

www.keyporter.com

Printed and bound in Canada
09 10 11 12 13 5 4 3 2 1

Library and Archives Canada Cataloguing in Publication

I love my hockey mom / Flyers Novice AE Team.

ISBN 978-1-55470-282-4

1. Hockey players--Family relationships--Ontario--Orangeville.
2. Mothers and sons. I. Flyers Novice AE Team (Hockey Team)

GV848.5.A1I3 2009   796.962092'271341   C2009-904721-7

this book is dedicated to all
hockey moms
with love and thanks.

contributors Cade B, Cameron M,
Carter T, Conner H, Dawson C, Ethan D, Ethan S,
Harrison M, Jacob S, Liam M, Myles H, Ranen D,
Richard W, Trevor A, Zach V

introduction

Being a hockey coach has provided me with the opportunity to teach—and learn from—some wonderful kids over the years. I have looked forward with anticipation to every game and practice, and savoured every moment: every win, every loss. I have also really enjoyed seeing the parents interacting with their children. Through the unique and very honest window that coaching sports opens, I have had a chance to witness these special relationships—intimate moments of loving, praising, scolding, teaching, and dreaming. There is almost no limit to what hockey parents will do for their kids.

And I guess that's how this project got started with our Novice rep team—I wanted to do something nice for the parents, for a change, on behalf of their kids. I wanted to do something that would give the kids an opportunity to show (and feel) love and appreciation, in this case for their moms.

With the help of a teacher, Jennifer Sutoski—who just happens to be the mom of one of our players—the project got underway. Jennifer worked with the players and encouraged them to think about their moms, and to remember the things for which they should be thankful. Their words, and the pictures they drew to accompany them, are honest, touching, surprising, and funny. I hope you enjoy them as much as we do.

The players remind us, with that special wisdom that only children seem to possess, that each moment is a memory to be filed away forever. These kids know what their moms have done for them—the efforts have not gone unnoticed.

I, too, love my hockey mom—a nursery school teacher who puts all her energy into helping other people. I appreciate the freedom she gave me as a child and as a player, the freedom to make mistakes without criticism. The best teachers (and coaches) know just what their kids need. Thanks, Mom!

jason howell Flyers Novice AE Coach

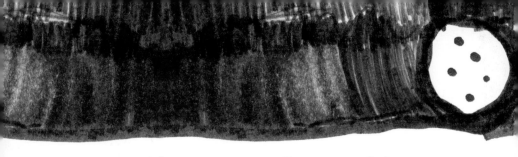

I remember my first set of skates: They were in the window of a shoemaker's shop, they had white tape on the toes, and I thought they were so cool. My Dad bought them for me. You never forget your first skates.

I remember my Mom waking me up at five in the morning, calling "Donald, Donald" quietly so as not to wake my brother. And off I would go by the light of a full moon.

I remember the first CCM stick my Dad brought home for me. I slept with it clutched in my arms.

I remember when I went away to play Junior A for the Barrie Flyers. The owner was a cheap guy and we had old equipment that

was **falling apart.** My hockey gloves were useless—they were full of holes. My Mom bought me a new pair. I was so proud to think that of all the moms that had sons on the team, the only mother who bothered to get gloves for protection was my Mom. That's Mother Love. When I look at the picture of me that still hangs in the arena in Barrie, I think of Mom and Dad and how they cared.

Del & Maud Cherry—they were the best. XOXO.

don cherry

harrison m.

i love my
hockey mom
for hugging
me when i lose

and she feeds me before games.

harrison m.

liam m.

i love my
hockey mom
because she lets me
shoot on her
in the driveway
for practice

and because
she will
sit or stand
in a

cold

arena while
i play.

i love my
hockey mom
because she skips
work for me

and she *kind of* helps me with **dressing.**

myles h.

trevor a.

i love my
hockey mom
because she airs
out my really

stinky

socks

and she
sometimes
comes to my
games.

trevor a.

dawson c.

i love my
hockey mom
because she taps me
on the helmet before
each game

and once
she banged
on the glass
so hard
that she

flattened

her ring.

dawson c.

i love my
hockey mom
because she
is my
best fan

and she
makes me
feel so
happy.

ranen d.

ethan d.

i love my
hockey mom
because she
takes me
swimming
after our
far away
tournaments

and she always cheers from the stands.

ethan d.

cade b.

i love my
hockey mom
because she makes
pizza
for dinner
before games

and she makes
room
for my equipment
in the garage
so it will not
stink in the house.

EASTON

cade b.

richard w.

i love my
hockey mom
even though
she goes crazy
by yelling the
loudest and
making the fans
move away

and she
makes me
beans,
bacon and
sausage.

richard w.

i love my hockey mom for sneaking

cameron m.

a kiss before every game

and once i forgot my
mouthguard and
she ran out to get one
10 minutes before
a game

and made it
back before the game.

cameron m.

i love my
hockey mom
because she
cries
when i get a
goal

conner h.

3 and once she drove hours in a snowstorm **scared** and felt like she was going to *pass out.*

conner h.

Slushie

pop
corn

choclate

zach v.

i **love** my
hockey mom
because she
buys me
snacks
after the
game

chips

and for being **cheerful** and **happy** at all my games.

zach v.

carter t.

i love my
hockey mom
because she
updates
my stats
on the computer

and

because she
takes me to

garage sales

to look for

goalie equipment.

jacob s.

i love my
hockey mom

for painting

my face

before my first
NHL game

and thanks,
mom
for holding my hat
when i was sick.
because i did not want to
miss *any* of that game.

jacob s.

ethan s.

i love my
hockey mom
even though she
covers
her face a lot
when i play,
because i am a
goalie

and my mom
loves hockey...
every game, until spring
when it gets warm

and then she
loves sum^m^{e}^{r}.

ethan s.

thanks, mom
i love you.